ACTIVE SHOOTER MITIGATION

A Training Guide for Houses of Worship

Kris P. Moloney

"If you want to be a sheepdog, you must make a conscious and moral decision every day to dedicate, equip and prepare yourself to thrive in that toxic, corrosive moment when the wolf comes knocking at the door."

—LTC (RET) DAVE GROSSMAN

Far too many people have lost their lives during active shooter events. This book is for the victims. It is from their tragedy that we learn to safeguard our churches from violence. May God continue to show His grace and mercy on their families and toward all of us in His service.

About the Author

Kris P. Moloney is a Police Officer with over 15 years of experience and a retired Army Captain and Company Commander. He has certifications in a number of specialties to include Crime Prevention and Security Assessments. In addition to his Bachelor's in Ministry and a Master's in Organizational Leadership from Northwestern College in St. Paul, he has served his church as a volunteer Safety Director for nearly a decade.

About the Coauthor

Malene A. Little earned a Master of Arts in English and a Master of Public Administration with a specialization in nonprofit management. She is dedicated to education at all levels and particularly grateful to work with Sheepdog Church Security in helping religious organizations create emergency plans.

Author's Acknowledgements

First, I would like to thank my wife, Rebecca, for patiently supporting me during this long process and believing in the vision and mission of Sheepdog Church Security.

I would like to thank LTC (ret) Dave Grossman along with my family and friends who encouraged me to write this book.

It would be impossible to thank all the people that made this book possible. However, among the numerous researchers, instructional designers, writers and editors, I would like to thank Malene Little, who can take a jumbled assortment of materials and combine them into a coherent book.

Finally, I want to thank the thousands of Christian Sheepdogs around the country who have supported Sheepdog Church Security. It was your input and resources that made this book possible. Thank you.

Kris P. Moloney
Visit my website at www.SheepdogChuchSecurity.net

Printed in the United States of America

First Printing: Dec 2018
Sheepdog Church Security

ISBN-9781791373481

SHEEPDOG CREED

AS A SHEEPDOG, I am a companion to shepherds and a protector of the flock. My fundamental calling is to support and protect the Church; to aid pastors in watching over their congregations (Acts 20:28), to safeguard lives and property, to maintain order; and to be an instrument for Peace and Security so all people may gather in Jesus' name to pray, worship and study in a sanctuary of safety and security (Psalm 5:11).

I will keep my life temperate and above reproach, maintaining self-control in the face of danger and temptation; I will be respectable and hospitable (1 Timothy 3:2); honoring others above myself and being constantly mindful of their welfare (Romans 12:10). I will be well-trained; technically and tactically proficient; disciplined, physically and mentally tough, ready to meet the challenges of my calling: executing justice and mercy for God.

To my congregation and pastor, I promise sustained, just and honorable support. I promise to be a professional, courteous and kind. I promise to always be ready to respond to emergency situations and to engage threats to the Church.

To my Lord and Master, I promise to find my Peace and Strength in You Alone, to Study Frequently, Pray Continuously, Worship Constantly and Love You Eternally, for I am a Servant and Guardian of the Kingdom of God (Psalm 28:7, Psalm 127:1).

CONTENTS

Icons

	A Closer Look: This icon indicates more details or an example.
	Definition: This icon indicates words/phrases that are defined.
	Download: This icon indicates a form or other resource to simplify your workload.
	In the Plan: This icon indicates information to use in creating plans or policies.
	Remember: This icon indicates an important reminder.
	Scripture: This icon indicates areas where scripture is used in the text.
	Tip: This icon indicates a tip for safety or a way to make your work easier.
	Warning: This icon indicates information on what to avoid.

KNOW THE WOLF

On November 5, 2017, a 26-year-old man entered the First Baptist Church in Sutherland Springs, Texas. He was carrying a gun and opened fire on the congregation, murdering 25 people and injuring 20 more before exiting the church[1]. A neighbor realized what was happening and shot the assailant twice[2]. As the assailant fled in his Ford Expedition, the neighbor pursued him with the help of Johnnie Langendorff. The assailant crashed after a high-speed chase and was found dead with three gunshot wounds, including the two shots from the neighbor and a self-inflicted head shot. The assailant's attack stemmed from his domestic situation; his mother-in-law and wife normally attended that church but were not present on the day of the attack (Bacon & Dearman, 2017; Crow, 2017). This attack was the deadliest on an American place of worship in modern history.

---

[1] Some reporters list 26 people killed because they include an unborn child as one of the victims; see McRary for an example.

[2] The neighbor does not wish to be named and has declined to speak with news sources. With respect to his privacy, we have not sought further information.

"I am sending you out like sheep among wolves. Therefore, be as shrewd as snakes and as innocent as doves" (Matthew 10:16, NIV).

At Sheepdog Church Security, we create Safety Ministries which Safety Teams are a part. A Church Safety Ministry is made up of church leadership and a Church Safety Team. They are responsible for the health and security of the church members and the prevention of damage and theft of church property. Their duties include administering first aid, monitoring donations, stopping an active shooter, and helping staff, volunteers, public, and first responders during an emergency. Full information on creating and training a Church Safety Ministry is in the Sheepdog Church Security's book *Defending the Flock: A Security Guide for Church Safety Directors.* This book (*Active Shooter Neutralization and Lockdown Drills for Houses of Worship: A Training Guide for Safety Directors*) focuses on preparing for active shooter events.

Some people think that preparing for an active shooter event means they are not putting their trust in God to protect them. However, a church can trust in God's protection while also working to prevent harm. Indeed, God has always instructed people to act reasonably to protect themselves: Jesus sent his followers "out like sheep among wolves" and told them to "therefore be as shrewd as snakes and as innocent as doves."

"While people are saying, 'Peace and safety,' destruction will come on them suddenly, as labor pains on a pregnant woman, and they will not escape" (1 Thessalonians 5:3, NIV).

Verbally affirming peace and safety is not adequate. Churches cannot allow destruction to come on them suddenly. Instead, church leaders must prepare members to be good people who are also ready for today's threats. A major threat is active shooter incidents.

The definition of "active shooter incidents" has evolved over time. They were first defined as "an individual actively engaged in killing or attempting to kill people in a confined and populated area," and the use of firearms is to be understood as the weapon in that definition (Blair & Schweit, 2014, p. 5). The Federal Bureau of Investigation (FBI) changed individual to individual(s) because some situations have multiple shooters; then, the FBI omitted "confined" because some incidents happened outside (Blair & Schweit, 2014, p. 5).

For our purposes, an active shooter is a person (or multiple people) who attack the church with deadly or potentially deadly force.

An active shooter could be a killer coming to church to shoot as many people possible or it could be an estranged spouse coming to church to kill his/her spouse.

Numbers Don't Lie

Texas State University and the FBI have been tracking active shooter incidents since 2000. In these studies, the FBI did not include gun accidents, suicides without homicide victims, or violence associated with gangs or drugs (Blair & Schweit, 2014, p. 5). Active shooter incidents are becoming more numerous and more dangerous.

Average Number of Casualties per Year
2000-2008, average = 48.4
2009-2017, average = 197.9

During 2000-2006, there were an average of 6.4 incidents annually, but that number rose to an average of 16.4 incidents each year during 2007-2013 (Blair & Schweit, 2014, p. 10).   In total there were 160 active shooter incidents between 2000 and 2013 with 1,043 casualties, not including shooters—an average of 74.5 each year (Blair & Schweit, 2014, p. 10).

Twenty incidents occurred in each 2014 and 2015 with a total of 231 casualties, not including shooters (Schweit, 2016, p. 2).   Twenty incidents occurred in 2016, and 30 incidents occurred in 2017 with a total of 943 casualties, more than triple the casualties of the previous two years (The Advanced Law Enforcement Rapid Response Training [ALERRT] Center at Texas State University and the Federal Bureau of Investigation [FBI], 2018, p. 1-2).

14

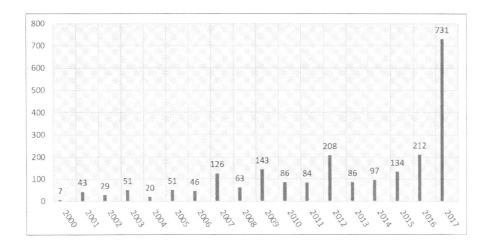

The locations of these attacks are most often a commercial or an educational site (ALERRT and FBI, 2018, p. 6; Blair & Schweit, 2014, p. 13; Schweit, 2016, pp. 4-5). However, churches are targeted too. Six of the 160 incidents from 2000-2013 were at a house of worship or a religiously-affiliated facility (Blair & Schweit, 2014, p. 13). Two of the 40 incidents in 2014 and 2015 were at a house of worship or a religiously-affiliated facility (Schweit, 2016, p. 5). Of the 50 incidents in 2016 and 2017, two occurred in houses of worship or religiously-affiliated facilities (ALERRT and FBI, 2018, p. 7).

15

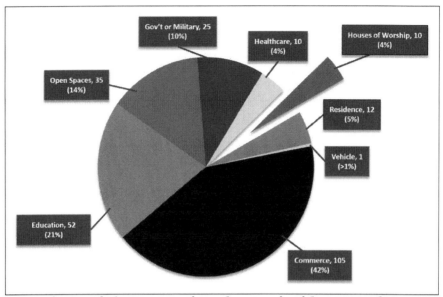

Locations of the 250 active shooter incidents analyzed by FBI for 2000-2017.

More disturbing than the number of active shooter incidents are the number of deadly force incidents, which include all deaths on church grounds. Carl Chinn (2018) has been tracking these statistics since 1999 and has counted 1705 incidents. This number is larger than the FBI's assessment because it includes all lethal violence, not just active shooters. For example, Chinn's numbers include the 2012 murder of Danny Kirk, pastor of Greater Sweethome Missionary Baptist Church in Forest Hills, Texas, who was beaten to death with an electric guitar (Pantazi & Crawford, 2012). Furthermore, Chinn's numbers correlate with the FBI's assessment that the threat is growing. Chinn counted 764 incidents between 2000-2013, but almost 77% of those

16

occurred in 2009 or later. This deadly trend continued, and Chinn counted 176 incidents in 2014, 248 in 2015, 246 in 2016, and 261 in 2017. Clearly, today's church members are in danger. One reason churches are attacked is because they are soft targets.

 A soft target is a person or location that is relatively unprotected or vulnerable.

Churches are soft targets for many reasons:
- Churches stand for religious truths many find narrow minded and/or offensive.
- Churches are open to the public with open access to anybody during services.
- Church service times are publicly known and consistent; even people who do not attend a church can easily learn service times.
- Many churches in the United States are gun-free zones and may not recognize their own vulnerability.
- Most churches have no Church Safety Ministry.

These are all reasons Sheepdog Church Security is committed to helping churches protect their people and property. The information is this book will help people to harden their churches.

Church leaders have begun to recognize the reality that an active shooter event may take place at their churches. This understanding resulted in an estimated 1,000 faith representatives attending Knox County Sheriff's Office church safety seminar on December 2, 2017 in Powell, Tennessee (McRary, 2017). Another 650 people attended a similar seminar on December 5, 2017 in the Dallas, Texas area (Ross, 2017).

Learning how to protect church members is of upmost importance. Indeed, Mike Gurley, retired Dallas policeman and principal of the security firm Teamworks Consulting Inc., urged people to use recent killings as a reason to train. Gurley referenced the November 5, 2017 shooting in Sutherland Springs, Texas when he said "The people on Nov. 5 were only doing one thing: They were gathering to worship. But they became the victims of a warped and twisted mind. We cannot let those people die in vain" (Ross, 2017). The purpose of this book is to help prevent further tragedies.

Characteristics of a Killer

Studies have shown that there is no typical shooter. Most of the shooters in the Texas State University and the FBI studies have been male and work alone. Of the 250 incidents in the three studies, only four involved more than one shooter. Further, there were only nine female shooters, and they were often part of husband and wife teams (ALERRT and FBI, 2018, p. 7; Blair & Schweit, 2014, p. 13; Schweit, 2016, p. 4).

Active shooters' motives can usually be organized into one of five themes: revenge, power, loyalty, terror, or profit (Fox & DeLateur, 2013, p. 127). Sometimes the shooter is not seeking a specific person but a type of person. For example, if a person sees himself as a victim of bullying, he may choose to kill people at school but not necessarily those who bullied him (Fox & DeLateur, 2013, p. 127). Similarly, a person who sees himself as unfairly passed over for a promotion may take revenge on people at the place of employment but not necessarily those people who made the decision.

Shooters often will not stop shooting until they have finished their mission. The Federal Bureau of Investigation (FBI, 2013) found that 70% of the incidents it reviewed were finished in five minutes or less (p. 8). Most shooters studied died in a shootout or by suicide. Fifty-seven of the shooters studies were killed by law enforcement and/or citizens. Fifty-two committed suicide before law enforcement arrived, and 40 after law enforcement arrived. Another 70 were apprehended by law enforcement or citizens (ALERRT and

FBI, 2018, p. 5; Blair & Schweit, 2014, p. 11; Schweit, 2016, p. 4).

 Do not use criminals' names.

Sheepdog Church Security does not use the names of criminals in its books. Scholars have found that after mass killings, there is a contagion effect which creates copycats (Towers, Gomez-Lievano, Khan, Mubayi, and Castillo-Chavez, 2015). On October 2, 2017, a group of 149 "scholars, professors, and law enforcement professionals" submitted an open letter asking media to not use shooters' names or pictures in coverage. Sometimes, would-be shooters are seeking the fame they think past seekers have found, and sometimes they become competitive and try to kill a higher number of victims ("Open Letter," 2017).

The Advanced Law Enforcement Rapid Response Training (ALERRT) Center at Texas State University works with the Federal Bureau of Investigation (FBI) in researching active shooters. The ALERRT system has created an organization called Don't Name Them (http://www.dontnamethem.org/) for these reasons. Therefore, Sheepdog Church Security omits needless information about shooters and limits material about the crimes themselves. Only information that will help church leaders prevent and prepare for attacks is included.

IMPORTANCE
OF PLANNING

U.S. Army Colonel Tom Kolditz explained that "no plan survives contact with the enemy" (qtd. in Heath & Heath, 2008, p. 25). What that means is that people cannot plan every step of an attack ahead of time. Enemies will surprise them, and weather, equipment failures, and other unexpected circumstances also play a role. However, the planning process is invaluable because it forces people to think about possible situations and outcomes (Heath & Heath, 2008, p. 26).

The U.S. Army also has a process called After-Action Review in which people analyze "what happened, why it happened, and how they can improve" (Hyatt, 2018, p. 68). This book will help church leadership plan for active shooter events and evaluate historical events to learn from the actions of past shooters. Of course, the purpose of this information is not to blame church leadership or victims but rather to find patterns in attackers' behavior so better decisions can be made in the future. All recommendations must be adapted to fit the church location, layout, size, and membership composition that is unique to each community.

Be alert to signs that someone is planning an act of violence because it is rare that people just snap. Instead, it is more likely he/she will have exhibited behaviors such as talking about violence, increasingly sharing information about domestic problems, displaying mood swings, or having worsening hygiene (FBI, n.d., p. 10). Often, killers plan their attacks far ahead of time, sometimes even months in advance (Fox & DeLateur, 2013, p. 126).

A good example of people being alert occurred on Sunday, February 18, 2018, when a concerned party alerted law enforcement about a man going through a divorce who had threatened to "shoot up a church [that his wife attended] and kill himself" (Jorge & Ferrier, 2018). When the man was arrested, he had an AR-15 and up to 1,5000 rounds of ammunition in his vehicle (Jorge & Ferrier, 2018).

This event illustrates why church staff, volunteers, members, and visitors should be vigilant. Often shooters' motivations include domestic violence, workplace violence, and hate crimes.

Domestic Violence

Domestic violence issues may extend from the home into the place of worship. Sixteen percent of deadly force incidents in a church were the result of "domestic spillover," and domestic abuse is a top reason for church shootings (Chinn, 2018; Shellnutt, 2017).

On November 5, 2017, in Fresno, California, a woman and her boyfriend were killed in their car by the woman's estranged husband (Wootson, 2017).

The same day, a shooter at First Baptist Church in Sutherland Springs, Texas, killed 25 people; his mother-in-law and wife normally attended the church (Bacon & Dearman, 2017; Crow, 2017).

According to a 2017 LifeWay survey, 45% of Protestant pastors do not have plans to respond to domestic violence situations (Shellnutt, 2017).

Hate Crimes

As a symbol of religion, churches are vulnerable to hate crimes. Churches can be targeted because of the type of church it is.

24

For example, in 2017 over 100 bomb threats were made on Jewish Community Centers, and mosques were vandalized, burned down, or otherwise attacked an average of twice each week (Burke, 2017; Coleman, 2017).

Churches can also be targeted for the ethnicity of its members. For example, churches with primarily African American members have known the fear of hate crimes since 1963 when the Ku Klux Klan bombed a Birmingham, Alabama church and killed four girls.

Churches can also be targeted because of religious differences, such as a stance on abortion (Burke, 2017). One study found that religious differences were the cause of 9% of church shootings while another found it only accounted for 6% (Burke, 2017). Religiously-motivated crimes are on the rise.

In 2003-2006 the percentage of religiously-motivated hate crimes was 10% out of all hate crimes (Walfield, Socia, and Powers, 2017, p. 149). That percentage increased to 21% for 2007-2011, and increased again to 28% by 2014 (Walfield, Socia, and Powers, 2017, p. 149).

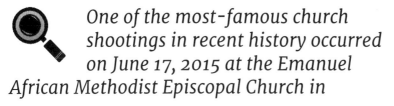
One of the most-famous church shootings in recent history occurred on June 17, 2015 at the Emanuel African Methodist Episcopal Church in

Charleston, South Carolina.

Around 9 pm, a 21-year-old male joined 12 churchgoers in a Bible study. Initially, he participated very little in the meeting; however, as the church members started to share scripture, he began to argue with them (CNN Wire, 2015). During the closing prayer, he pulled out a gun and started shooting (CNN Wire, 2015; Sanchez & Payne, 2015). During the shooting church members pleaded with him to stop. He swore at them and used racially charged language (CNN Wire, 2015).

By the time the assailant was done, he had killed nine people and injured one (Costa, Bever, Freedom du Lac, and Horwitz, 2015). He was arrested the next morning during a traffic stop in Shelby, North Carolina, approximately 250 miles from the church (Costa, Bever, Freedom du Lac, and Horwitz, 2015). The shooter's motive was his hatred of African Americans; he wanted to start a "race war" (CNN Wire, 2015).

Workplace Violence

As a place of employment, churches are also vulnerable to workplace violence. Each year more than 1,600 people are murdered, more than 2,000,000 people are assaulted, and more than 6,000,000 people are threatened at their places of work (American Crime Prevention Institute [ACPI], 2012, p. 395).

There are several types of people who commit workplace violence: third-party intruders such as an angry ex-husband or an emotionally disturbed person, disgruntled workers who feel cheated for not having received a promotion or raise, and assailants whose primary motive is to commit a robbery or hate crime (ACPI, 2012, p. 396).

There are several conditions which make workplace violence more likely: chronic labor/management disputes, numerous injury claims, under staffing, demands for overtime, many anxious personnel, aggressive management styles, and environmental pressures (ACPI, 2012, p. 398).

PREPARING THE CHUCH

This chapter covers information that all church members (staff, volunteers, regular attendees, and guests) need to know during an active shooter incident. This information should be shared with anyone in the church and this chapter is written as an instruction guide.

Your church is working to protect you from danger. However, sometimes danger will occur. One type of threat is an active shooter incident. An active shooter incident is when someone uses a firearm to intentionally shoot people in a populated area (Blair & Schweit, 2014, p. 5). If an active shooter incident occurs, there are three steps to survival: take flight (run), take cover (hide), and take action (fight). These three steps are detailed below.

28

Take Flight (Run)

Evacuation is the most important element during an active shooter event because if people can escape, they are safe. Even though people sometimes think there is a second attacker waiting at exit points to ambush them, only four of the 250 incidents in the 2000-2017 data involved more than one shooter (ALERRT and FBI, 2018, p. 5; Blair & Schweit, 2014, p. 7; Schweit, 2016, p. 4).

 During evacuation, consider all exits, not just the door in which you entered.

Many people only think about the doors they use frequently, so think about multiple escape routes using all doors and windows. Leave possessions behind (e.g. laptops, backpacks, purses, etc.). If possible, take your phone so you can call for help.

Help evacuate others if you can (especially children or people with mobility issues). However, leave without them if they will not go. Leave the seriously wounded behind (United States Department of Homeland Security [DHS], 2008, p. 3). This advice is easier to follow in a commercial setting such as a mall or airport where you may not know other potential victims. It is much harder to apply this advice when you have your family—perhaps including small children—and friends with you at church.

Just as people are taught to put on their own oxygen masks first in an airplane emergency, people need to protect themselves in a violent situation. It must be a personal decision to sacrifice yourself by acting as a shield for other potential victims.

If it is possible to get out of the building, try to prevent others from going into the danger zone because they may not know that an attack is happening (DHS, 2008, p. 3). Your church should hold trainings and drills on how to respond during an active shooter incident. During the drills, practice using escape routes such as back doors and windows. Do not use your car because automobiles bottleneck at exit points and, with the increased stress you are feeling, accidents and injuries are likely.

 A reunification point is an area to which people evacuate that is

removed from the setting of the active shooter.

Your church leaders will have identified reunification points away from the church where you should evacuate to during the drills and real events. At the reunification area, find cover and concealment (see below). Do not gather into large groups. At the reunification point, contact law enforcement even if it is possible someone else has already called in the attack. Practice this step during the drills because in a panic, it is common for people to forget to hit send after dialing 911.

Provide as much information as possible, including the following:
- shooter's location inside the building,
- number of shooters,
- physical description of shooter(s),
- weapons being used, and
- information on potential victims (DHS, 2008, p. 5).

If it is dangerous to speak, leave the line open to 911 so the dispatcher can hear what is going on. Stay on the line until the dispatcher hangs up. Stay at the location until law enforcement directs you to leave (DHS, 2008, p. 5).

Take Cover (Hide)

If it is not possible to take flight, then **take cover** (i.e. hide).

 Cover is anything that will stop a bullet, such as a cinderblock wall or many layers of metal and wood. Most interior walls are sheetrock and studs, so they will not stop bullets.

 Concealment is anything that will hide a person from view but is not necessarily cover; concealment includes large plants, interior walls, pews, and office furniture.

Find places where the intruder is less likely to find people. Hide behind something that will stop bullets. For example, the best place to hide is a room that has a lockable door and little to no glass. If there is an interior window, close and cover it, and move as far away from it as possible.

Try to maintain freedom of movement. Rooms with a second door leading to another area of the church or a window out of the church give you evacuation options. If the active shooter is breaking down one door, you can evacuate through the other exit. When hiding, do the following:

- Try to find rooms that lock such as bathrooms, offices, or classrooms. Do not open the door until law enforcement has said it is safe to come out.
- Lock and blockade doors and other entryways. Use furniture, books, chairs, and anything else that could fall onto the attacker if he tries to get into the room.
- Turn off all lights.
- Stay quiet and silence phones' noises, including vibrations.
- Do not huddle together in a large group. Instead, spread out throughout the room and hide behind large items that may provide cover.

Avoid the fishbowl effect, which is when the attacker can shoot into a room with large or many

windows to kill a crowd of people. Use furniture to barricade interior doors (DHS, 2008, p. 3).

During drills, brainstorm what cover, concealment, blockades, and weapons are available in each room. When you are hiding, do the following:

1. Find cover and concealment.
2. Block the door.
3. Find weapons in case you have to fight.
4. If you are not certain law enforcement has been contacted, call them. Provide as much information as possible, including the shooter's/shooters' location inside the building, number of shooters, physical description of shooter(s), weapons being used, and information on potential victims (DHS, 2008, p. 5).
5. If it is dangerous to speak, leave the line open to 911 so the dispatcher can hear what is going on. Stay on the line until the dispatcher hangs up.
6. Stay at the location until law enforcement directs you to leave (DHS, 2008, p. 5).

Practice these steps with church personnel and members during drills.

34

Take Action (Fight)

If an active shooter is determined, then he/she will get into your church. Escape and evasion should always be first actions, but it might be necessary to take action and engage the shooter (i.e. fight).

 For most people, running and hiding are going to be the best options.

Passive or stationary targets are easy victims. Compliance is dangerous, and submission to active shooters rarely pays off.

During the 2007 Virginia Tech shooting, students were advised by the university "Please stay put" (CNN, 2016). Students sat in their chairs as the attacker shot one at a time (Grossman, 2012). Even as he reloaded, the students just sat there waiting to be killed (Grossman, 2012). Likewise, the victims at the Charleston Church begged for their lives, but the killer coldly shot them (CNN Wire, 2015).

Waiting for police is not a sufficient defense strategy for an active shooter incident. Active shooter situations are often over before law enforcement arrives (DHS, 2008, p. 2). In the incidents for which the duration was known, almost 70% were finished in five minutes or less (Blair & Schweit, 2014, p. 8).

If staff, volunteers, or church members are in imminent danger, do everything possible to disrupt or incapacitate the active shooter. Be aggressive and follow these steps:
- Turn chaos and mayhem into an advantage and try to escape the area.
- Cause sensory overload and distractions by yelling.
- Throw whatever is available at the intruder's face (shoes, coins, Bibles, hymnals).
- Find anything that can be used as a weapon (a candle holder, fire extinguisher, solid metal cross)
- Work with others to swarm the intruder. If you're hiding with others, figure out how you can disable him if he enters your area. Keep the plan simple. Some people can throw things or otherwise distract him while others swarm the intruder, grabbing his limbs. Be committed to disabling the shooter. Do what you have to do!

- Consider using non-lethal weapons, such as defensive spray.

Never comply with an active shooter's demands. Recent events show active shooters are not interested in making deals or negotiating. They just want to murder as many people as they can.

During drills, the Church Safety Team should teach you how to swarm an active shooter with one or two people grabbing each of the shooter's arms and legs. Remove and secure the person's weapon when you gain the upper hand. During drills, the Church Safety Team should also teach you how to use medical equipment and administer first aid.

Citizen engagement is crucial. Sixty percent of the active shooter incidents between 2000-2013 ended before police arrived; in 21 of those incidents (13.1%), unarmed citizens were able to stop the shooters (Blair & Schweit, 2014, pp. 6, 11). In six (20%) of the incidents in 2014 and 2015, the shooters were stopped by citizens (Schweit, 2016, p. 2). In eight (16%) of the incidents in 2016 and 2017, the shooters were stopped by citizens (ALERRT and FBI, 2018, p. 2). Always run or hide first, but fighting can also save lives.

 It is okay to do use force to defend yourself and others in an attack.

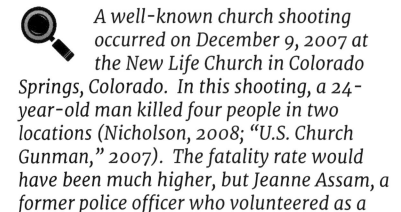 *A well-known church shooting occurred on December 9, 2007 at the New Life Church in Colorado Springs, Colorado. In this shooting, a 24-year-old man killed four people in two locations (Nicholson, 2008; "U.S. Church Gunman," 2007). The fatality rate would have been much higher, but Jeanne Assam, a former police officer who volunteered as a security guard, shot the attacker multiple times, putting him down. The man then killed himself ("U.S. Church Gunman," 2007).*

When First Responders Arrive

Police are there to eliminate the threat—not to tend to the wounded or anxious. Police might push you away or trip you to more quickly get to the intruder. Officers may shout commands, use pepper spray or tear gas, and/or push you to the ground for your safety (DHS, 2008, p. 5).

When police arrive, do the following:

- Keep hands up and empty with fingers spread. People holding cell phones or wallets can be accidentally shot because police think they have a weapon.
- Avoid sudden movements, and don't yell.
- Don't ask questions or grab officers.
- Exit from where the officers are entering because they have cleared that area.
- Do not run away from the police, and do not run directly at the police.
- Treat injured people when it is safe.
- Maintain lockdown until police say it is safe to unlock doors.
- Stay at the church until the police have interviewed people and given permission for people to leave.
- If necessary, go to reunification area to find family members and friends.
- Follow any other orders the police give.

If the intruder has been contained before police arrive, holster any weapons if it is safe to do so. Notify police that the intruder has been contained. Police may not receive the update, so holster weapons so that police will not accidentally mistake you for the intruder. If the police come while the intruder is being covered by a someone with a weapon, have him/her drop or holster the weapon when the police arrive.

When first responders arrive, help medical personnel if requested. Do not get in their way if help is not requested. Let the Church Safety Team decide if it is safe to treat the shooter; he may have other weapons or explosives. Additional officers and medical personnel will arrive after the initial officers have ensured the threat is eliminated (DHS, 2008, p. 5).

SAFETY TEAM RESPONSE

This chapter covers information that all Church Safety Team members need to know during an active shooter incident. This chapter is written as an instruction guide.

Teams

The Church Safety Team is responsible for the health and security of the church's members and property. Church Safety Team members should know everything the public knows and the information in this chapter. Church Safety Team members must be familiarized with all equipment that church leadership purchases. Equipment includes monitoring systems, public-address systems and other communication equipment such as hand-held radios,

41

secondary locking devices, evacuation equipment, and medical equipment. It is possible that all this equipment will be necessary during an active shooter incident.

In addition, during an active shooter incident, people will be looking to leaders, staff, and Church Safety Team members for guidance. Remain calm and direct people to evacuation routes and secured areas. Even frequent attendees of the church may panic and become completely lost. More information about specific responses to an active shooter incident will be covered in this chapter.

If there are enough people on the Church Safety Team, the team may be divided into Medical and Security sub teams. However, all Church Safety Team members should be cross-trained, so that everyone knows how to react in an emergency.

The Church Safety Security sub team may be divided into a containment team, engagement team, and congregation team. Again, all teams should be cross-trained because it is impossible to know what duties a person may have to perform during an active shooter incident.

It is also important to note that we never really know how people will react in a violent intruder situation. Some of your team members may display great courage while others may be nearly frozen in fear. By cross training, we maximize our team by giving them a fall back responsibility (containment) that can save a lot of lives.

 A containment team member evacuates people from the area and initiates lockdown.

During an emergency, the containment team verbally alerts people of the threat with instructions to either evacuate or go into lockdown. They will have to decide what is the best course of action for people to take based on the situation.

Generally, if the active killer is close and people cannot evacuate safely, then a lockdown should be initiated. This is likely to be the best choice for classrooms with younger children.

Evacuation is likely the best choice for people caught out in the open and they are at immediate risk of serious injury or death. This is also a good option for people who can evacuate quickly without putting themselves in the line of fire.

Once the appropriate procedure is initiated, the containment team members take a defensible position at an entry way to a populated area. The goal is to defend a large number of people by placing themselves between the active killer and the protected people. (e.g. waiting in a hallway leading to the children's area) The team member should use the best cover and concealment available and train their weapon to the most likely avenue of approach.

The best-case scenario is the killer's avenue of approach with contain a fatal funnel like a hallway or a closed door. Should the active killer enter the fatal funnel, the team member can engage to neutralize the threat.

This also serves as a way to control the killer's movements and potentially drive them toward the engagement team. For example, they may retreat from the containment team's gun fire into the engagement team's line of fire.

 An engagement team member tries to de-escalate the situation and/or prepares to use force.

44

The engagement team is responsible for neutralizing the threat (i.e. getting the person to stop shooting). The engagement team should move toward the target to neutralize the threat. Along the way, advise others to go into lockdown or evacuate. Everyone except the engagement team should move away from the sound of gunshots. The engagement team should continue to move *toward* the sound of gunshots using cover and concealment. More information about specific responses to an active shooter incident will be covered in this chapter.

Be careful while going around corners. The engagement team's task is to neutralize the threat using whatever force is necessary. The engagement team uses concealment and cover to take down the intruder. If lesser levels of force can be used to end the situation, they should be use instead of deadly force.

 The Congregation Team is the undercover branch of your safety team.

The Congregation Team's primary responsibility is to blend into the congregation and respond to life-threatening incidents in the sanctuary. While neutralizing an active shooter in the sanctuary is on the top of their list of responsibilities, they are also responsible for threats against the pastor (executive protection), disruptive or potentially violent people (including protestors), and life-threatening medical incidents within the sanctuary.

The Congregation Team should be strategically positioned in the sanctuary in plain clothes. From this location they can immediately respond and neutralize a threat that originates as he/she enters the sanctuary. The team should attempt to remain as anonymous as possible; however, if the situation garners an immediate response, they can intervene immediately to prevent injury.

 Fatal funnels are narrow areas such as hallways, stairways, or doors that prevent the active shooter from moving side to side. In the December 2007 shooting in Colorado Springs, Colorado, Carl Chinn positioned himself in the hallway with other team members set up to engage the shooter, sort of as a hasty ambush (Sheepdog Seminars, 2015).

Containment and engagement teams work together to utilize fatal funnels in an attack. Containment team members lock doors and block areas to limit the shooter's movements and route the intruder to the engagement team. For example, if the children's area is in a room down a hallway, then the containment team can lock areas going to that hallway or use furniture to narrow the area. This action protects the children. At the same time, it can allow the engagement team to ambush the shooter. This example shows why it is so important to use the church's floor plans in creating emergency responses and practicing these actions regularly.

As a Church Safety Team member, you should know what equipment is available and how to work it. All interior doors should have locksets. Often, locksets are available so that they require a key from the outside, but the inside can be opened without a key. These are especially good for meeting fire codes. Locked doors save lives. In the 2012 shooting at the Sandy Hook Elementary School in Newtown, Connecticut, no one who was in a locked room was shot (Dorn, Dorn, Satterly, Shepherd, and Nguyen, 2013).

Unfortunately, what frequently happens with locked doors is that people get annoyed by constantly having to open the door to latecomers or people who stepped out to use the restroom, so they stop the door from latching. That practice means that the room is not secure and thus not safe. Likewise, if people are unsure how to use the lock, it is useless. At Sandy Hook, 20 people were killed because the rooms were not locked down (Dorn, Dorn, Satterly, Shepherd, and Nguyen, 2013). Therefore, be vigilant about ensuring doors are shut and locked as appropriate. Make sure everyone knows how to use secondary lock systems if the church has them. (Church leadership will determine what device—if any—is needed and will train you on how to use them.)

It is important to work with church leadership to create procedures and emergency plans. Your input is valuable because you have unique perspectives on what will work for you and your team members.

Plans

The following information should be included in church plans and practices.

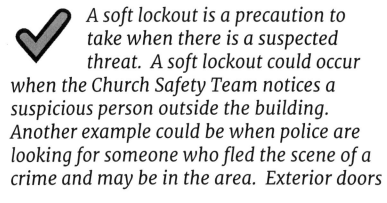 *A soft lockout is a precaution to take when there is a suspected threat. A soft lockout could occur when the Church Safety Team notices a suspicious person outside the building. Another example could be when police are looking for someone who fled the scene of a crime and may be in the area. Exterior doors*

are locked and monitored, but normal operations continue during a soft lockout. At any point, the Church Safety Team can put the church into lockout.

Public schools are a good example of how simple it can be to have the facility in a constant soft lockout. For example, schools have exterior doors locked during the school day; however, the doors can be opened from the inside without unlocking them. Likewise, it is easy for churches to monitor doors to allow access to latecomers. Many schools also have video monitoring equipment, so that parents and other visitors must identify themselves before they gain access to the building. Schools are easily put into lockout by closing and locking interior doors.

✔ *A lockout is when there is an active threat outside the church. For example, if a shooter is outside the building or a nearby church is attacked, put the church into a lockout. Exterior access points need to be secured and people should be moved to the center of the building away from doors and windows.*

During a lockout, Church Safety Team members should do the following:

1. Lock all access doors and vehicle gates. Do not open perimeter doors or gates to anyone who is not authorized to enter the property.
2. Monitor exterior doors and security cameras.
3. If the attacker gets close enough, issue a churchwide alert according to the policies set forth by church leadership. This alert may be on a public-address system and may include notifications on cell phones, Facebook, etc. A good announcement will inform people of the threat and its location: "Lockout, lockout, lockout. Threat at nearby bank. Lockout, lockout, lockout." Of course, you should change the location as necessary.
4. Call 911 if the attacker comes near.
5. Do not evacuate because the attacker might take people hostage.
6. Be prepared to go into lockdown if the attacker gets into the building.
7. Remain in lockout until advised by law enforcement that the area is safe.

A soft lockdown is a precaution to take when a suspicious person enters the church or is wandering the hallways. Interior doors are closed and locked, but the normal church operations continue.

✔ *A lockdown is when interior rooms, such as those leading into children's areas or classrooms, are locked are locked (and ideally barricaded) with people sheltering inside them. If an active shooter is in the building, the church should go into lockdown.*

A lockdown plan will require the Church Safety Team to do the following:

1. Issue a churchwide alert according to the policies set forth by church leadership. This alert may be on a public-address system and may include notifications on cell phones, Facebook, etc. A good announcement will inform people of the threat and its location: "Lockdown, lockdown, lockdown. Active Shooter in the lobby. Lockdown, lockdown, lockdown." Of course, you should change the location as necessary.
2. Call 911.
3. Help people take flight (run/evacuate).
4. Depending on where the attacker is, help people take cover (hide) by getting behind cover when

possible and finding concealment where there is no cover.

5. Make sure all interior rooms are locked with lights out and curtains closed.
6. Advise people to spread around rooms, be quiet, silence cell phones, stay low to the ground, and do not use lights.
7. If church leadership has installed secondary locking devices, use them.
8. Monitor cameras and be prepared to take action (fight).
9. The engagement team should position the team so that they can neutralize the shooter as quickly as possible. Remember to use fatal funnels as possible.
10. Remain in lockdown until advised by police that the area is safe.

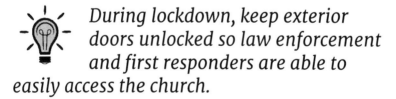 *During lockdown, keep exterior doors unlocked so law enforcement and first responders are able to easily access the church.*

 An enhanced lockdown is when the

building is in lockdown mode, but Church Safety Team members help people evacuate.

Enhanced lockdown plans should include an evacuation component. If people can leave the building and go to the reunification areas, that may be a better plan than having them hide inside the church. Alternately—for example, if the shooter is on the west side of the building and people are on the east side—it may work better to evacuate people rather than have them hide inside the church. Often, church interior doors do not have locks and are not good quality (e.g. a hollow, wooden door that is easily broken), so it is better to get people to the reunification points.

Some churches are always in a safety posture, which includes elements of a lockout and a lockdown. Exterior doors are locked and monitored. Interior doors are locked but may be propped open. At any time, the Church Safety Team member can easily call for a lockout so that the congregation is not alarmed and there is no interference with normal operations. If necessary, the Church Safety Team can also initiate a lockdown.

Example Situations

Sheepdog Church Security encourages After-Action Review to determine how different decisions could have resulted in a better outcome; <u>no blame</u> is bestowed on the churches or victims in the analysis of or suggestions for the following situations. If the shooting starts in a hallway, there may not be any way to take cover. Additionally, people will probably be rushing around, trying to evacuate.

Parking Lot

One situation to prepare for is if the shooter is in the parking lot. The shooter at the Burnette Chapel Church in Tennessee sat outside in the parking lot before entering the church. He made only one fatal shot; Melanie Crow Smith left the church and went to the parking lot alone. If the Church Safety Team members had patrolled the parking lot, they could have noticed him sitting there and locked the door. Even if a person has no nefarious plans, situational awareness is helpful. A person may be alone in the car waiting to give a member a ride home, praying on his own, or just trying to get free Wi-Fi. However, seeing a suspicious vehicle might prompt the Church Safety Team to write down a description of the vehicle and the license plate in case something unexpected happens later, such as a robbery later in the week.

In the case of the shooter at the Burnette Chapel Church, the Church Safety Team could have locked the doors and engaged him with firearms before he entered the church. It would be important to have the Church Safety Team go into a prone position (i.e. lying on stomachs) to be smaller targets and engage the intruder at doorways. Perhaps the Church Safety Team could have been aware when people were starting to leave the church and watched to ensure members made it safely to their cars. This practice can help people even in poor weather; if the parking lot is icy and a person falls, the Church Safety Team members can help the person back up.

Consider how the Church Safety Team will deal with it if the intruder is outside trying to get in and people are outside the church and running back for cover. If the intruder is far enough away, it may be safe to let them in. However, if the intruder is too close and could gain entrance at the same time, a team member may have to make the hard call of locking out the people. At some point the door will have to be closed to safeguard the greatest number of people inside the church. Failure to close the doors could result in a much higher number of people being killed or wounded. No one wants to make the call of leaving people in a dangerous situation, but the greater number must be protected inside. If there are a lot of people outside, perhaps the Church Safety Team should send members out to protect people and engage the shooter in the parking lot. Average police response time in America is six minutes (Moloney, 2017). Ideally, the procedures will give you at least that much time.

Potentially Violent Person

A second situation to prepare for is if a potentially violent person has been identified. When dealing with a potentially violent person, immediately call 911 for police response. Do not be afraid to call the police. It is far better to have police respond to the church before the person acts out in violence. If you use the Sheepdog Church Security radio codes, this situation is a Code Orange 911. "Code Orange" means "a violent person or potentially violent person" has been identified. 911 is an enhancement code meaning "call police." An example transmission would be, "Code Orange 911 in lobby. I say again, Code Orange 911 in lobby." When possible and safe, use verbal de-escalation. If it's working, keep at it. If verbal de-escalation is not working and it is relatively safe to do so, use self-defense techniques. Swarm the subject if feasible. Consider the use of non-lethal weapons, such as defensive spray.

As a last resort, use the force reasonably necessary and in accordance with the law to neutralize the threat. Position armed persons where they have clear lines of sight to the subject. You should consider what's behind the subject. You don't want to shoot towards a crowd. Armed persons should

56

consider cover, concealment, and maneuverability. They should ask themselves, "If I am taking heavy fire, how can I escape?"

Sudden Active Shooter

A third situation may be if an active shooter incident happens suddenly. If the shooter is already in the church and among the people, consider how the church members can best be protected. Don't use codes for an active killer. Instead, send this transmission (but change the location as appropriate): "Lockdown, lockdown, lockdown. Active Killer in the lobby. Active Killer in the lobby. Lockdown, lockdown, lockdown."

The containment team should move through the crowd and clear space, helping people evacuate or go into lockdown. This should be done quietly without arousing suspicion. If the intruder is already in the church, only the interior rooms of the building should be locked. Leave the exterior doors unlocked, so responding police can get in.

The engagement team should move toward the target to neutralize the threat. Everyone but the engagement team should move as far away from the sound of gunshots as possible. The engagement team should continue to move toward the sound of gunshots using cover and concealment. It will be chaos, so there might not be a clear line of sight.

Everyone will likely be running, so it might not be possible to identify the shooter immediately. For example, maybe it will work to put people at back of sanctuary and shoot intruder from either side. Be careful while going around corners. The engagement team's task is to neutralize the threat using whatever force is necessary.

The engagement team should move in formation toward the shooter, utilizing cover. It is important to note the presence of any body armor, or the possibility of explosive devices attached to the shooter. At that point a designated team member should move forward in small three-to-five-second rushes, utilizing cover until he/she closes on the shooter enough to engage, or until the last available cover between them and the shooter. Then, from cover and with aimed shots, the team member should fire shots aimed center mass until the shooter drops.

Once the shooter drops, the team member should remain in place with visual contact on the shooter. The remaining team members will then advance to cover the area. The team should not approach the shooter until they are sure that he/she is neutralized. The team should stay on alert for the possibility of a second shooter or explosive devices left throughout the building, carried by the shooter, or wired (e.g. a   suicide   vest).

LEADERSHIP RESPONSIBILITIES

Church leadership should know all the information for the public and the Church Safety Team. In addition, church leadership is in charge of creating and implementing the policies and plans to keep everyone safe. There are seven steps to prevent an attack or mitigate the damage done by an attacker. The steps need to be done in this order, but some steps may be recursive (e.g. an emergency plan is made, equipment is purchased, and then the plan is updated to include the new equipment).

1. Perform a facility assessment.
2. Create policies.
3. Create and train teams.
4. Develop emergency plans.
5. Purchase equipment.
6. Train public and conduct drills.
7. Hold meetings to assess threats.

These steps will help organizations create emergency action plans for active shooters.

Performing a Facility Assessment

First, conduct a facility assessment by identifying access points, potential security vulnerabilities, and communication systems. Access control is especially important because if an intruder cannot get into the church, the attack cannot happen. Access points include all routes of ingress, as well as locations in the church that can serve as a shelter or safe area. Access points include doors, windows, roof latches, skylights, hallways, interior offices, and classrooms. Evaluate how access points are locked and secured. Even an action as simple as placing a large planter in front of the church can prevent automobiles from crashing into the building.

 Download: *Facility Assessment*

Some churches choose to have a safety posture during all church events. The doors are locked but not closed; they can be closed quickly if a warning is issued. Often, most people are already in the church by the time the sermon starts.

Church Safety Team members can watch doors to allow latecomers entrance if necessary. Monitoring access points is particularly helpful because then the Church Safety Team members can assess latecomers for threats. For example, Church Safety Team members can ask themselves the following questions:

- Is the person carrying anything?
- Does the person seem flustered or nervous?
- Is this person known by the Church Safety Team?

Having this additional awareness can prevent some attacks. For example, the shooter at the Burnette Chapel Church of Christ in Antioch, Tennessee was wearing a mask and holding guns when he entered the church (Sterling, Lynch, Grinberg, 2017).

Access Points

Evaluate all access points. Access points include doors, windows, roof latches, sunroofs, etc. Evaluate how doors and windows are locked and secured. Identify problems by asking questions in the Facility Assessment form (available for download as an Excel file and PDF). Exterior doors should be locked at all times. If locking all exterior doors is not possible (for example during a service), then have someone monitor the entrances.

61

It is important to not only evaluate the church property but also any problems people have in getting to church. For example, if there are frequent attacks on people who walk to church, maybe the church can coordinate carpool services, so it is safer.

All access points should be able to lock. To reduce confusion and the number of keys people have to carry, consider keying all public interior doors (e.g. nursery, kitchen, classrooms) with the same key. Different locksets can be used for private offices. Of course, locks should be changed when there is a change in personnel. Another option is to have a keypad and change the codes as needed. To control access, give keys and codes to only the people who need them. If there are vulnerable access points, numerous devices are available to fortify them. (See the section on Target Hardening.)

Installing security gates and fences discourage vandalism and loitering because people have a difficult time even getting onto the property. Adequate lighting and clear lines of sight are also necessary to prevent crime. Ensure there are no dark areas or large bushes in which people can hide. Cameras are recommended in areas that are not regularly patrolled by the Church Safety Team. For example, if the Church Safety Team remains inside during services, then monitoring the parking lot with cameras is important because vandals and thieves can take advantage of the empty cars. These criminals even know how much time they will have because service times are often public knowledge.

Situational awareness can be a big deterrence of crime or help to solve it after the fact. When a man was burglarizing cars on April 1, 2018 (Easter Sunday), a witness noticed him looking into cars and recorded his actions. A church member confronted the man and he fled, but thanks to the witness who recorded him, the thief was apprehended and charged with the crime (Huffstutler. 2018).

Security Vulnerabilities

In addition to inspecting access points, it is important to evaluate monitoring systems. Maybe a secretary or receptionist working in the office is enough to monitor the one door that is open during the week, but Church Safety Team members need to be aware of all access points during the busiest times. Security components, such as closed-circuit televisions, intrusion alarm systems, and perimeter lighting, should also be evaluated. Check how they are functioning and whether all personnel know how to use the systems. Purchase additional components if required.

Communication

The next step in the facility assessment is to identify existing communication strategies and devices. In an emergency, plan to use all available means of communication to provide as much information as possible to a wide audience. Two-way radios, text messaging, a public address (PA) system, digital signage, the Internet, Twitter, Facebook, etc. are all viable communication options. Communication systems must be in place to notify everyone. Think about how you will notify people in every area. For example, how to notify people in the sanctuary and classrooms if a fire starts in the kitchen. If Virginia Tech had notified people of the first incident, the shooter would not have been able to continue the massacre (Fretz, 2007).

Medical Training

All Church Safety Team members, staff, and frequent volunteers should receive medical training including information on how to use equipment to treat injuries, how to control severe bleeding, how to use tourniquets, how to perform cardiopulmonary resuscitation (CPR), and how to use an automated external defibrillator if someone goes into cardiac arrest. It may even be worth the time and money to have Church Safety Team members trained as Emergency Medical Technicians, so they can perform life-saving techniques after an active shooter incident. The American Red Cross holds classes around the country on CPR, first aid, using automated external defibrillators, and more. Check https://www.redcross.org/take-a-class to see when and where your team can be trained.

Further training should be done to teach Church Safety Team members how to triage after an active shooter incident. Triage is an evaluation method which assesses victims and categorizes them into colors to designate who needs treatment first. The most commonly used type of triage is Simple Triage and Rapid Treatment (START) (Radiation Emergency Medical Management [REMM], 2018).

The START system categorizes victims into four color categories:
- **Black** for expectant,
- **Red** for immediate,
- **Yellow** for delayed, and
- **Green** for minor (REMM, 2018).

People are classified as black if they are unlikely to survive. They should be given comfort including pain relief if possible. People who have problems with airways, breathing, or their circulation should be classified as red and need treatment within an hour. People who are severely injured but should

65

last a couple hours without intervention should be classified as yellow. People who can walk should be classified as green (REMM, 2018).

The focus has to be put on the RED. Perform life-saving first aid to people in need of immediate help. Yellows and Greens are lower priority so as many lives as possible are saved.

 If people are wounded in an active shooter incident, let law enforcement take the lead in notifying families. Law enforcement personnel are trained on how to deliver the news in the most sensitive way. However, they may need help in reaching families, so aid them in any way they request.

Creating Policies

Church leadership must approve all policies. Some of these policies will be affected by the laws in the city and state in which the church is located. It is the responsibility of the church to research the appropriate laws in its area. One such policy should be to only use the minimum amount of force necessary to stop an aggressor. Also decide if Church Safety Team members should be armed or able to use restraints.

 Your policies must conform to applicable state and local laws of your area.

Church leadership should ensure Church Safety Team members are trained in all approved defense methods including (if applicable) verbal de-escalation, hand-to-hand combat, escort techniques, restraints, using pepper spray, and lethal weapons. Church leadership should also determine how to choose which Church Safety Team members should be armed (if any) and how they will be trained. Private instructors are often able to help with training. At a minimum, annual qualifications are recommended.

Church Safety Team members should be physically fit because they may have to run, jump, climb, squat, and otherwise move in uncomfortable positions in order to confront aggressors. They should also be emotionally stable and spiritually mature. In the worst case, a team member may have to take a life to stop an attacker. That situation is a heavy burden on anyone, and the decision must be made by the team member in the moment and not because of policy or training.

Communication Policies

Communication is extremely important. Sheepdog Church Security recommends that the team members use earphones or ear buds. They will work with all radios. Using earphones will mean that when there are things coming out over the radio, the radios are not bothering anyone. The pastor does not want to hear your radio going off in the middle of service. Also, emergency calls about a fire in the kitchen or some other minor emergency won't alarm the people because they just won't hear it. The following information is meant to guide you in creating your own policies.

Radios need to be worn and turned on at the beginning of each shift and used throughout the shift. Radios must remain on campus unless there's an off-campus event. Radios are to be maintained per manufacturer's instructions. Radios are regulated and can be heard throughout the campus and beyond, so casual conversations, profanity, inappropriate remarks, and music are prohibited. All violators are subject to disciplinary measures.

Keep transmissions short. For a long conversation, use the telephone. If you need to discuss something with a specific person, begin transmission with the name of the person you are calling followed by your name. One example would be "Pete, this is Bob." Pete's response would be "Go ahead, Bob." When you're done with your conversation, sign off.

An example would be "Bob out." That's how we clear all transmissions, even unanswered ones. This way, if somebody else is on the radio and they're waiting to get to say something, they can hear that you are done. Of course, only interrupt transmissions in the case of an emergency.

Use plain English with the radios except for codes discussed below. The more you listen and use the radio, you'll hear how others use it and get the feel. For first expressions

- "Go ahead," means "Send your message."
- "Copy," means "The message was received and understood."
- "Say again" means "Retransmit your message." Perhaps you were doing something else and didn't clearly hear the message.
- "Stand by" means "I heard your message but please wait."
- "Affirmative" or "Yes" means "Yes."
- "Negative" or "No" means "No."
- "Do you copy?" means "Do you understand?"
- "Unreadable" means you can't understand the person who transmitted the message (i.e. you don't know what was said because the message was garbled due to a technological problem).
- "Disregard" means "Don't pay any attention to the last message."

The following approved codes are the exception to the plain English rule and are to protect the congregation. If you have a minor fire and say over the radios, "There's a fire in the kitchen," people may hear that and understandably become alarmed. You may alter these codes so they are unique to your church. Individualizing the codes means that anyone who reads this book does not have access to your unique codes.

- Code Red is a fire emergency.
- Code Blue is a medical emergency.
- Code Pink is a missing or lost child.
- Code Orange is an actively disruptive or combative person.
- Code Yellow is a suspicious person.
- Code Green is a cash or offerings escort.
- 911 is an enhancement code which means respond quickly and call local law enforcement. (In using this code, you would include the other code: "911 Code Orange 911" would be an example.)

Do not have too many codes because people may forget what each means and have delays in their responses. In emergencies, delays can be deadly.

USE OF FORCE CONTINUUM

L aw enforcement agencies have policies and expectations that guide their use of force in resolving violent situations. An example of a use of force continuum policy is as follows:

- Presence. Officer presence deters violence, and no force used.
- Verbal De-escalation. The officers make statements such as "Let me see your license and registration." They may increase volume and issue commands such as "Stop."
- Empty-Handed Control. The officer may restrain the individual through grabs, punches, and kicks.
- Less-Lethal Methods. The officer may immobilize an individual with a baton, chemical (such as

pepper spray), or a Conducted Energy Device (such as a taser).

- Lethal Force. An officer may use deadly force (such as using a firearm) to stop an individual. (National Institute of Justice, 2009).

During an active shooter incident, lethal force may be necessary to prevent the attacker from causing serious bodily harm or death. However, use of force should be limited to the minimum amount of force necessary to stop the actions of the aggressor. If there is any way to stop the aggressor using less than lethal force, the Church Safety Team should do that instead. For example, if there is an aggressive person who is yelling and disruptive, then try to use verbal de-escalation instead. (More information about verbal de-escalation is available in Sheepdog Church Security's book *Defending the Flock: A Security Guide for Church Safety Directors*.)

Laws

The United States made provisions so that people can act in self-defense, i.e., use force (even deadly force) to protect themselves, other people, or property. The laws explained below can also be applied to Church Safety Team members defending their congregations and church property. Most states also include language so that people who act in self-defense have immunity from criminal prosecution and may

7ᵛ

even be entitled to compensation for attorney's fees and lost income if prosecuted (Reinhart, 2007, p. 3).

Laws vary from state to state, and it is best to check applicable state legislation to know specific rights. The following are general guidelines about using self-defense. Self-defense laws generally require that force be used only when there is an imminent (immediate) physical threat to oneself or a third person (such as a spouse or child). It is not justified to use force against someone who makes a verbal attack with no "accompanying threat of immediate physical harm" ("Self-Defense Overview," 2016).

 Reasonable belief refers to what the person who uses self-defense could have reasonably believed under the circumstances. For example, if a stranger seems to be suddenly about to strike your head, it is reasonable to defend yourself. If that stranger is only to trying to swat away a bee, your reaction can still be viewed as reasonable ("Self-Defense Overview," 2016).

If a person has an unreasonable belief of threat, he or she could be prosecuted for assault or even murder but may plead "imperfect self-defense" and have the charges and penalties reduced ("Self-Defense Overview," 2016). Not all states

73

recognize this defense. This criterion means that when someone acts in self-defense, he or she must react in a way that matches the threat. If someone is attacked but his or her life is not threatened, the defender cannot respond with deadly force. Likewise, if the attacker is neutralized easily, then continuing to fight the attacker would be considered retaliation and not self-defense ("Self-Defense Overview," 2016).

Duty to Retreat laws are used in many states and mean that a person must try to escape from an attacker before using force as self-defense. Some states stipulate that a person may use force as self-defense but may not use deadly force without first trying to flee the situation ("Self-Defense Overview," 2016). No duty to flee in NC

The Castle Doctrine is a common law in many states that allows people to defend themselves in their homes. The concept comes from English Common Law and the idea that "one's abode is a special area in which one enjoys certain protections and immunities" (State of New Jersey, 2008). The concept got applies in NC, but NOT that NAme

74

its name from Florida lobbyist Marion P. Hammer and comes from the phrase "one's home is one's castle" (Reinhart, 2007, p. 1).

The Castle Doctrine allows defenders to not retreat as is required by many states (Randall and DeBoer, 2012, p. 1). The Castle Doctrine extends not only to protecting oneself and family or guests from bodily harm but also to preventing theft of property (Randall & DeBoer, 2012, p. 1). Weapons should not be used to stop the theft of church property or funds unless there is also a threat to the safety of someone during the theft.

Stand-your-ground laws have been passed by twenty states and allow people who are legally in a location to use force without first attempting to retreat (Randall & DeBoer, 2012, p. 2).

Yes in NC

It is legally defensible to protect others but only to the extent that the person would legally be able to defend himself/herself. This means that if two people are fighting, a third person may legally come to one of the party's defense and use force to stop an assault. The third person can only use as much force as necessary to stop the assault, so lethal force would not be justified if the assailant could have been diverted by verbal de-escalation ("Defense of Others," 2016).

75

"If a thief is caught breaking in at night and is struck a fatal blow, the defender is not guilty of bloodshed; but if it happens after sunrise, the defender is guilty of bloodshed" (Exodus 22:2-3; New International Version).

The Bible tells us not to use lethal force only to stop theft unless we fear for our lives. By law, people are allowed to use non-lethal force to stop the theft of property or to immediately recover stolen property, but that deadly force can only be used to "defend a person from the use of or imminent use of deadly physical force or infliction or imminent infliction of great bodily harm" (Reinhart, 2007, p. 4).

Restraints and Chemicals

Church Safety Team members will not use any type of restraint (including handcuffs) on any person involved in an altercation in the church unless it is determined that the use of a restraint is required to prevent serious injury to the person or someone else. Once a person is placed in restraints, a citizen's arrest has taken place. The security team members are responsible for the safety of the person in restraints.

NOT IN NY

76

Restraints may be permitted in situations such as the following. A violent person has assaulted a church member with a knife and has been stopped by the Church Safety Team. The person continues to fight and there is a high likelihood of additional injury to a church member or a team member. It is clear that the aggressor would immediately attempt to reengage the fight if released. Restrain the person until the police arrive to take him/her into custody. Note that once you have restrained a person, you are legally responsible for his/her welfare. This responsibility must not be taken lightly.

Church Safety Team members will not use any type of chemical (including pepper spray) on any person involved in an altercation in the church unless it is determined that the use of a chemical is required to prevent serious injury.

Firearms

The use of weapons as a security measure is a controversial topic. There is no doubt that former police officer Jeanne Assam saved lives when she shot and wounded the shooter at New Life Church in 2007 (Eckstrom, 2008, p. 17). Brady Boyd, New Life Church senior pastor; John Ross, security director at Dallas's Oak Cliff Bible Fellowship; and Scott Thumma, author of *Beyond Megachurch Myths*, see armed guards as necessary (Eckstrom, 2008, p. 17). In contrast,

George Battle Jr., the senior bishop of the African Methodist Episcopal Zion Church, argued that Isaiah 54:17, which reads "no weapon formed against you shall prosper," means that guns should not be used for protection either because they are formed against us and thus shall not prosper in use as a defense (Banks, 2015, p. 17). Pastor Kyle Childress (2016) of Austin Heights Baptist Church argued fiercely against guns in the church and told his pulpit, "When I went down into the waters of baptism, I did not come out to strap on a gun. I came out entering into the life of the crucified and resurrected Jesus Christ" (p. 11).

Marc Brooks, a deputy sheriff and chief instructor for Protective Services Training and Consultants, reported that firearms are not always necessary for protecting the church (MacDonald, 2009, p. 14). Brooks said, "It just requires that you're alert and that you're in shape and that you're able to protect your pastor" (MacDonald, 2009, p. 14). Rick Anderson, founder of Church Security Solutions, expounded upon this idea by advising people to look for indications that the person may be planning an attack including "a stranger who appears nervous, avoids eye contact and cuts casual conversation short" (MacDonald, 2009, p. 14).

Indeed, being armed may not even be a deterrent to a violent intruder as he/she is most likely intending to die in the situation (MacDonald, 2009, p. 14). Eric Spacek, senior risk manager for GuideOne Insurance reported that allowing armed guards or members can also "increase the liability exposure for the organization" (MacDonald, 2009, p. 14). The federal government cannot dictate if churches allow armed guards or armed congregations, but it does give churches guidelines on facing a shooter and advised those people in danger to "run, hide or fight" (Markoe, 2013, p. 14).

 Church Safety Team leaders should approve the use of any weapons before the team is allowed to carry them.

The security team leader or pastoral staff leader should issue a policy identifying the following:
- approved defensive weapons,
- the requirements for certification in the use of each type of weapon, and
- the list of people who are approved to carry each kind of weapon.

Anyone who carries a weapon without prior authorization should be dismissed from the team.

If Church Safety Team members will carry firearms, those members' skills should be evaluated at least annually. Firearms must be registered according to local, state, and federal regulations. People who use firearms should regularly practice using them. In addition to increasing muscle memory of using the weapon, practice should involve knowledge of limitations of the weapon and tactical shooting. Encourage members also practice in shooting ranges frequently.

Have a professional firearms instructor train the Safety Team members on how to accurately fire weapons, including while they are moving. The training should focus on short-range combat because most of the attacks will be made within the church, not a long distance from the church. As with all of these skills, Church Safety Team members should practice regularly to ensure muscle memory and fast response to dangerous situations.

Church Safety Team members who carry firearms should conceal them.

 Put in the firearms policy that display or printing of firearms is prohibited.

Printing means the outline or shape of the firearm can be seen through the clothing. The reason for this policy is that many people attending church may become uncomfortable or at least distracted by someone open carrying a firearm. The purpose of church is to make disciples, and distracting people by displaying firearms is counterproductive. The second reason that display or printing is prohibited is tactical. An attacker will target Church Safety Team members with guns first to eliminate threats; it is better to surprise the attacker regarding who has a firearm.

Drawing from the holster may seem trivial, but it is an important drill. Most concealed carry holsters are not like what law enforcement officers wear but, instead, are built for comfort and concealment. Therefore, Church Safety Team members should practice drawing an empty firearm in front of a mirror. Have them practice hundreds of times so that they can quickly draw from any position (sitting, kneeling, lying on their backs, lying on their sides, lying on their stomachs, etc.).

Remind Church Safety Team members about the difference between cover and concealment. (See definitions in Chapter 2.) Have them find areas of cover and concealment throughout the church and practice shooting from those locations. Again, make sure they get practice shooting from all positions: kneeling, standing, squatting, and lying on their backs, stomachs, and sides.

To prevent injury to other people, Church Safety Team members should ensure that discharging the weapon will not cause another person to be injured. Training should include shoot/don't shoot scenarios because it is most likely that attacks will occur when the church is full of innocent people.

Church Safety Team members will have only milliseconds to determine if the target is the threat or a scared bystander. Check with local gun clubs or law enforcement to see where this type of training is offered.

 When training in the church, use airsoft guns because they are safe for every area of the church. The bullets may sting, but pain is a good teacher. Airsoft guns are also better than paintball guns because the latter make a mess, and people will spend a lot of time cleaning the paint off everything.

Creating and Training Teams

The third step is to create and train teams. Generally, a church has three options for creating its Church Safety Team: hire off-duty law enforcement personnel, hire professional security guards from an agency, or create own security guard service (GuideOne, 2018). If the Church Safety Team will be made of volunteers, consider which members of the church have backgrounds in police, military, or security (Stetzer, 2017).

The location of Church Safety Team members in relation to the active shooter may determine how each person must react, so cross-train all Church Safety Team members. Additionally, people do not know how they will respond in an actual attack and may not be able to perform engagement activities when they think they can. At a minimum, Church Safety Team members should understand how to contain the threat and engage the attacker. Form containment and engagement teams. (See information under chapter 3 for more information on these teams.)

Any person who responds to an active shooter situation is putting his/her life in great danger. This response must be an individual decision and not dictated by policy or training. In evaluating who should work on the teams, Sheepdog Church Security recommends that

- all team members be trained for tactical situations including verbal de-escalation and hand-to-hand combat,
- all armed members meet the minimum legal requirements to carry a firearm,
- all armed members are familiar with the use of force laws and policy,
- all armed members are sufficiently trained to use their firearms in a tactical situation, and
- all armed members regularly practice their shooting (at a firing range, for example).

It is the responsibility of the church and individual Church Safety Team members to ensure that these recommendations are met.

 Pointing a firearm at a person has legal implications, and it may trigger a violent response. It also slows the ability to respond with self-defense techniques because transitioning to self-defense techniques requires spending several seconds holstering the weapon. Additionally, if the team member is too close to the shooter, the gun can turn the situation into a deadly force altercation. Many police officers are shot with their own guns because they took it out when too near the subject (Federal Bureau of Investigation, n.d.).

Developing Emergency Plans

To create emergency plans, first view a detailed site map or floor plan of the church. Know which doors lock and which doors need additional security. Identify places of vulnerability such as long hallways.

Refer to the Facility Assessment download for specific questions to ask while conducting the facility assessment. Create battle plans with details such as "If he's in the lobby, Safety member #1 approaches down hallway #1. Member #2 approaches from sanctuary." It is not possible to plan for every situation, but the church is safer with each plan and practice.

Based on the facility assessment, develop lockout, safety posture, lockdown, and enhanced lockdown plans. Use the floor plans to make a clear plan of action for each room of the church. Make it easy to understand what to do in different types of emergencies. People need to know the best way to evacuate from the room and the best way to hide in the room. It is important to realize that the fastest evacuation route may not be the safest; a back hallway may take longer but it may be safer than trying to cross a larger area such as a dining room.

Identify several reunification points in case any are unusable at the time they are needed. Each reunification should not be in line of sight of the church. (If there is an active shooter, he/she should not be able to see the reunification point from the church.) The reunification points should be at least 1000 feet from the church.

Do not use the same reunification points that are used for fire evacuation areas. In the Jonesboro school shooter situation of 1998, which had two attackers, one pulled the fire alarm and then both shot people as they made their way to the pre-determined fire evacuation areas (Goodwyn, 2018). Likewise, terrorists will place improvised explosive devices (IEDs) to stop vehicles and also place IEDs in the area the vehicle will be stopped. Because attackers are more likely to know the location fire evacuation areas than active shooter reunification areas, it is best to plan multiple areas for both types of evacuation.

 Create a placard to put on the door of each room explaining what to do if an emergency happens while someone is in the room.

Include information such as barricade devices available in the room and how to use locks and secondary locking devices. Consider having brochures printed to give to church members. Include information about reunification points and what to do after an attack. The information should not be not secret; everyone from the oldest member to the first-time visitor needs to know what to do if the church is under attack.

 This brochure with Run, Hide, and Fight information is a good

addition to your own information with evacuation routes and tips for each room.

Special Considerations

In the emergency plans, consider what will be done to help people with special needs. If someone is visually or hearing impaired, that person still needs to know there is an emergency. This reason is why the church should purchase several types of alerts. An audible alarm (or even just the public-address system) can inform visually impaired people, but a visual alarm will be beneficial to someone who cannot hear. This strobe light (https://www.visiplex.com/product/led-strobe-light/) is an example of a visual alarm.

Likewise, people who have cognitive disabilities may need help processing the alarms. People who use wheelchairs may need support during evacuation. While creating the emergency plans, consider making numerous doors handicap accessible so that no one is trapped inside.

Another area to consider is the children's area. If the adult-to-child ratio is too low for the adults to carry infants and small children out of the church, then perhaps it is a good idea to purchase evacuation aids (see the section on purchasing equipment). The easiest way to make sure each room is evacuated is to assign 2-3 people to each room so that even if one Church Safety Team member is working as a containment member, there is someone responsible for helping to evacuate or help hide the people in these special rooms.

A good idea is to have a codeword that changes daily. When the church is in lockdown, a Church Safety Team member will have to give the codeword to the people in the nursery and/or classroom(s) before the doors are unlocked. This codeword can be written each day on a whiteboard inside the nursery where visitors cannot see it but staff and volunteers can easily check that the Church Safety Team member has the right word. Smaller churches may choose to rely on personal recognition. There is no greater form of identification than actually knowing the person as a friend or colleague.

After an Attack

Create a plan to resume normal operations once the lockout or lockdown is over. Know how the church will notify people the lockout/lockdown is over. If church leadership was not at the church during the attack, have members of the Church Safety Team who were present explain to leaders what happened. After an attack, someone with public relations experience should hold a press conference to answer questions. Church Safety Team members should not answer questions or allow themselves to be interviewed unless they have been asked to do so by church leaders.

Know ahead of time how the building will be cleaned or repaired if necessary. Know if the church will resume operations that day (if possible) or wait until the next day to start scheduled activities. If the church is unusable for more than a day or two, know alternate locations where the church can hold services. Perhaps another church in the area would allow use of its facility during hours it is not performing its own services.

Know how to connect people with resources if they have mental health problems. The Substance Abuse and Mental Health Services Administration offers a Disaster Distress Helpline (1-800-985-5990), which offers 24/7, 365 free crisis counseling. The American Red Cross provides Disaster Mental Health training, and it may be worth the cost and time to have some of the Church Safety Team members trained in that service.

Once the initial emotional response has dissipated, the Church Safety Team should conduct an After-Action Review to identify what parts of the plans and training were most and least helpful. Assess where the team was most effective and what could be done differently should another attack occur. Always evaluate and revise emergency plans as new information (including efficacy during an emergency) is available.

Purchasing Equipment

This information is for church leadership to make decisions on equipment to purchase. As you are completing your emergency plans, make a list of equipment to purchase for target hardening, communication systems, emergency supplies, and medical supplies. Types of frequently needed equipment are below with examples. You are encouraged to do your own research to ensure the equipment you purchase meets the needs of your church.

Target Hardening

Target hardening is making a place more difficult to attack. The Bible has several examples of people following God's commands to fortify their barricades.

 "He strengthened their defences and put commanders in them, with supplies of food, olive oil and wine. He put shields and spears in all the cities, and made them very strong" (2 Chronicles 11:11-12, New International Version).

Bosch (https://us.boschsecurity.com) offers access control systems to replace keyed entries. There are also numerous devices are available to act as secondary locking devices for doors. 123 Lock-Down Latch, Classroom Rapid Lockdown System, and Lock Blok are devices that are installed to be permanent parts of the door which are used with existing locksets so doors can be constantly locked and easily engaged. There are also devices that temporarily block door movement such as CinchLock, Bearacade, BOLO Stick, and Nightlock.

123 Lock-Down Latch (http://www.123lock-downlatch.com) is made of aluminum and steel and can be retrofitted to existing doors. It uses a rubber bumper to stop the door from closing so people can easily go in and out of the door. It enables the lockset to be constantly locked, so that people can go into lockdown without going outside or even looking for keys. 123 Lock-Down Latch costs $45/each.

The Classroom Rapid Lockdown System (http://www.classroomsecure.com) is a device fit over an existing doorknob. It stops the doors from shutting completely and allows people to merely push or pull open doors when in the unlocked position. When it is necessary to go into lockdown, the door requires one quick motion from the inside to put it into a locked position. The price is $95/each.

Lock BLOK (http://www.doorblok.com/lockblok.html) has a two-part design made of ABS plastic and neoprene and can be used on any type of doors. The device allows the lockset to be locked while blocking the door from closing so people can easily enter and exit. When a lockdown is needed, the slide is moved away from the edge of the door. Depending on the number of Lock Bloks ordered, the cost is between $9.90-11/each.

Tempshield (https://tempshieldschools.com) are magnetic coverings for doors and windows that allow instructors to hide the room's interior from view in seconds. The cost depends on the size of coverings and quantity your location needs.

The CinchLock (https://www.cinchlock.com) is a temporary device which blocks doors from opening toward the device. It grips the door and holds it shut. The device is not a permanent part of the door, so storage may be an issue. The CinchLock can be installed in 30 seconds and costs between $50-$110 depending on the type of door being blocked.

Bearacade Lockdown Response System (https://doorbearacade.com) prevents both inward and outward opening doors from opening because it slides under the door and anchors a pin to a preinstalled hole in the floor. This device's main distinction is its optional "reflective External Notification Panel," which lets administrators know which rooms are secure. The device is not a permanent part of the door, so storage may be an issue. The Bearacade Lockdown Response System is $59 each.

93

BOLO Stick (https://bolostick.com) is an easy system which is installed to the bottom of a door and allows it to be anchored a pin to a preinstalled hole in the floor. These devices resist more than two tons of pressure and are quick to be implemented. The pin is not a permanent part of the door, but it is small enough to hang on a wall near the door. Each BOLO Stick is about $60.

NIGHTLOCK Lockdown 1 (https://nightlock.com) also secures the door to the floor and is suitable for both inward and outward swinging doors. The lock function is not always attached to the door, but it is small and can be hung on a wall or a desk. NIGHTLOCK Lockdown 2 is only for outward swinging doors and uses the door frame for reinforcement rather than the floor. They are also quick to put into lockdown. The prices range from $60-$70/each.

Communication Systems

Communication systems are essential in preparing for any emergency. There are several types of communication systems such as emergency alerts, public-address systems, and handsets. Prices vary depending on the type and number of products you purchase.

Bosch (https://us.boschsecurity.com) has numerable useful communication products including fire alarms, intruder alerts, and public-address systems.

Radios can be expensive. Motorola is a brand Sheepdog Church Security recommends for two-way radios because they are reliable and there is wide selection to meet each organization's needs. A reasonable radio with a range that will work for most churches is Motorola's TALKABOUT® MT350R. The only problem is the sound quality can be poor so when people get excited and start to yell a little bit, their voices get garbled. There are also many expensive radios you can purchase. The Black Diamond CE450 is recommended. These are a lot better because the quality is better and the distance for which people are using them is appropriate with this model. Read the user's guide for any radios your church purchases.

Motorola has now has WAVE OnCloud (https://www.waveoncloud.com), which enables smart phones to be used as push-to-talk devices (i.e. the two-way radios most people use) as well as allowing the traditional push-to-talk devices to interact with people using smart phones.

There are several emergency mass notifications systems which can send messages to numerous people at once about active shooter incidents, administrative updates, or church closings due to weather. AlertFind (https://alertfind.com) is a cloud-based application which allows an administrator to instantly send alerts as phone calls, e-mails, and text messages. Omnilert (https://www.omnilert.com) is executable from a computer, smart phone, or Apple Watch and allows the user to send detailed messages, including previously written emergency plans. OnSolve (https://www.onsolve.com/) is used by government agencies and educational institutions to send mass notifications about safety issues such as active shooter incidents and more pedestrian updates such as communication about staff scheduling. Warnable (http://warnable.com) is an electronic platform which uses push notifications, texts, and e-mails to alert people to situations and walk them through the predetermined responses.

Emergency Supplies

Purchase "bug-out kits" and place them throughout the church. Each bug-out kit should include emergency water and food supplies, medical supplies (see below), extra ammunition, and anything else that might be needed in an emergency. Train all staff and volunteers on how to use the contents of the bug-out kits.

Emergency supplies also include evacuation equipment. There are several types of evacuation aids that are beneficial. Depending on the needs of the people in the church, research what makes the most sense. This evacuation chair (http://www.hospitalaids.co.uk/products/evacu-b) allows six infants to be transported at once and even goes up and down stairs. Additional equipment can be purchased as needed at http://www.sure-line.com/evacuation-equipment/.

Medical Supplies

Medical supply bags should include flashlights, rolls of bandage, tourniquets, and pressure dressing. QuikClot (https://quikclot.com/QuikClot) is a pressure dressing that contains kaolin to stop bleeding by accelerating natural clotting. Medical supply bags should be in conspicuous locations, so that they are easy to retrieve and use. Consider hanging small medical supply bags near fire extinguishers or putting them under the ends of pews.

Training and Conducting Drills

Training and drills include training the Church Safety Team and training everyone else (e.g. staff, volunteers, members, public). Start by training the Church Safety Team because emergency plans may change based on the members' input. The Church Safety Team must be comfortable with all aspects of the emergency plans before anyone else is trained.

Train the Church Safety Team

Train the Church Safety Team in both medical responses and security. This training will make sure that the team understands how to communicate risk, how to help evacuate people, how to use equipment including secondary locking devices, how to help people hide, and how to engage with the attacker if necessary. Training should be ongoing, but it is especially important for the team to conduct drills on its own before involving the church staff, volunteers, and members. Do not conduct a church-wide drill until the Church Safety Team knows everything first.

Conduct drills with the Church Safety Team by going to every area of the church and thinking of all scenarios. Analyze the best places for concealment and cover in every room. Think like an intruder and plan how to attack in each part of the church (e.g. nursery, Sunday School area, Bible study area, kitchen and snack areas, classrooms, offices, etc.).

The location of team members in relation to the active shooter may dictate how each member must react during the incident (e.g. a containment team member may have to work as an engagement team member or vice versa).

Always cross-train the Church Safety Team members.

As the Church Safety Team completes its drills, the members should write down and combine notes the evacuation routes, safe rooms, best areas for cover and concealment in each room of the church, communication plans for the special-needs members, additional help for the children's area, etc. The Church Safety Team will probably have ideas on how to solve problems such as planning communication efforts and evacuation routes for children and special needs members with physical, emotional, or cognitive problems.

In addition to creating procedures for each area of the church, practice verbal de-escalation and hand-to-hand combat. Create contingency plans in case there are staff missing that day or other unusual circumstances. Practice scenarios should include situations when the Church Safety Team is not firing back. The correct procedure or tactic is the one that works for the preference and expertise of the people who create it. Go through all the example situations in chapter three.

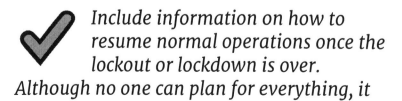 *Include information on how to resume normal operations once the lockout or lockdown is over.*
Although no one can plan for everything, it

is best to do as much planning as possible before an actual attack.

Conducting Drills

In addition to training the Church Safety Team, it is important to conduct drills with staff, volunteers, members, and people with even nominal attendance.

 Never conduct a drill without advance notice. People will panic if the drill is a surprise.

Before conducting a public drill, get support from church leadership. Explain to the church leaders why it is necessary to hold a drill. Share information from this book if it will help. The pastor and other leaders need to understand that this type of drill is just as important as fire drills (and arguably more so because of the frequency of the threat). Utilize local law enforcement when designing training exercises. Police can teach people how to recognize the sound of gunshots, react quickly when gunshots are heard and/or when a shooting is witnessed, and evacuate the area (DHS, 2008, p. 6).

Teach staff, volunteers, members, and the public all responses: lockout, lockdown, and enhanced lockdown. They will need time to practice what they have learned. Make sure they understand everything about how to respond during a lockdown. During a lockdown drill, people need to know survival tactics.

Childcare workers will need special training to know how to lock and barricade the rooms, silence devices, turn off lights, draw curtains, help the children hide and be quiet, and keep count of everyone. Childcare workers may also need to practice using evacuation aids. The children themselves may not understand the importance of the drills or why they need to move quickly and be quiet, so it is likely they will need additional practice sessions in which their parents can help. Have small drills with the children and childcare workers before attempting a church-wide drill.

Next, set a date to hold the church-wide drill. Work with church leaders to set a date to conduct the drill. Ask if first responders have anyone they can spare to help facilitate the drill. Notify first responders even if they cannot be there, so that they do not dispatch if someone mistakes the drill for a real active shooter event.

Make sure church members know the date and time of the drill, so they can react calmly and learn the procedures. This step may take weeks or months. Church members must understand evacuation routes and how to take flight, take cover, call 911, take action, treat the injured, and react when first responders arrive. The drill must be low stress and low intensity, so that the church members can see it as a learning process and not a test. Conduct drills regularly, at least on an annual basis, so that people can remember what to do if there is an emergency.

Holding Meetings

The final step in preventing an attack is to conduct regular meetings to evaluate threats. Form a threat assessment team that meets regularly to discuss people who may be experiencing crisis. The intention is not to gossip about the person but to instead identify who is suffering from a personal crisis, so the church can offer counseling and assistance.

It's critically important to understand why people become disruptive. Disruptive behavior is often the result of a personal crisis. A personal crisis happens when a person perceives an event or situation has exceeded his/her ability to cope with the problem and the emotional anguish becomes intolerable. There are several causes of personal crisis:

- family problems: a marriage falling apart, teenagers acting out, arguments with in-laws, etc.;

- financial problems: home may be in foreclosure, may have lost a job, may not be able to feed family or pay bills;
- substance abuse: alcoholism and addiction can put a great deal of strain on people;
- medical conditions: chronic pain, a serious medical diagnosis, or even terminal illness can change people's personalities and behavior; and/or
- mental illness: mental illness can also contribute to verbally combative behaviors.

A person who has a personal crisis is not weak in faith or character. Everybody has hard times, so compassion is necessary. It is important to engage in intentional ministering so that the broken and lost are given the help they need.

Before someone becomes verbally combative or physically violent, he/she usually exhibits several warning signs. Warning signs can include changes in behavior such as disrespect for authority, crying, poor hygiene, incompetent job performance, and changes in energy levels (Canadian Centre for Occupational Health and Safety, 2014). The person can also exhibit physical signs such as shaking, sweating, restlessness, a loud voice, and inappropriate physical boundaries (Canadian Centre for Occupational Health and Safety, 2014). Often, no one person sees the entire picture. It is only after leaders share information that a clear picture of what is going on in a person's life emerges.

The Canadian Centre of Occupational Health and Safety (2014) explains that the meetings should include discussions of the following:

- a history of violence, including an interest in weapons or past violent acts;
- threatening behavior, such as excessive phone calls or threatening to hurt someone;
- intimidating behavior, such as being impulsive, easily frustrated, or uncooperative;
- an increase in personal stress, such as addiction, family issues, or financial problems;
- negative personality traits, such as being suspicious or blaming others for mistakes; and
- changes in mood or behavior, such as expressing hopelessness or showing agitation or anxiety (Canadian Centre for Occupational Health and Safety, 2014).

If the team identifies someone with these signs, have ministry reach out to that person to help him/her before the problems result in a disruption.

Consider situations such as if there is a new middle-aged woman who is going through divorce and has two children, maybe her husband will try to abduct children during church services. Sometimes religious women do not even see violence against them as wrong but instead try to understand it as part of "God's plan" (Shellnutt, 2017).

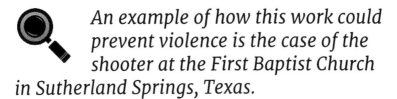 *An example of how this work could prevent violence is the case of the shooter at the First Baptist Church in Sutherland Springs, Texas.*

The attacker sent his mother-in-law threatening messages. If the church had known and encouraged her report to the crime, perhaps the shooter would not have been able to attack the church. Of course, this is just conjecture, but the point is that assessing threats can help the church be more prepared. As always, these suggestions are not meant to blame the churches that were victimized. Instead, it is important to learn from those situations to help churches identify ways to prevent attacks.

These meetings are also a good time to evaluate unmet needs in the church. Perhaps school is starting and several parents cannot afford to buy school supplies. Maybe the church can connect those parents with charity organizations or otherwise help them. These meetings do not have to solely be about assessing potential violence. The point is to intentionally minister to people in need.

These meetings are also an appropriate time to review emergency plans and make changes as necessary. If a renovation has just been done to the church, then the plans need to be updated to include information on new access points. If a new elevator has been installed, find out if it is classified as a fire elevator. If there has been turnover in the staff, designate who will fulfill which roles in each type of emergency. Consider changing locks and/or keycodes if someone who had access to those keys/keycodes has left the church. Always review plans to ensure that they meet the needs of the church in the present.

Conclusion

Active shooter incidents are a problem that is increasing. Using the ideas in this book will enable your church to prevent and prepare for attacks. Several steps are necessary. Perform a facility assessment, create policies, create and train a Church Safety Team, develop emergency plans, purchase equipment, train people and conduct drills, and hold meetings to regularly assess threats.

Now for a bit of caution. If you are like so many others who are working diligently to safeguard your congregation, you should be aware of a number of pitfalls.

The first pitfall is the overwhelming desire to apply everything in this book immediately. While that is a noble goal, the truth is that developing a strong Active Shooter Response program at your church will take time. This can be very frustrating but doing something correctly is just as important, if not more important, than doing it fast.

I highly suggest, identify the quick and easy wins. For example, it doesn't take a lot of time to create a lockdown procedure for the children's ministries. (Eg, close and lock doors, turn of lights, hide around the room, remain silent) Even the smallest steps in the right direction will make your congregation safer.

The second pitfall is introducing an Active Shooter Response program before your church and its leaders are ready. This can be a catastrophic mistake. Every church is different, but many are hesitant if not totally against an Active Shooter Response program. There are many reasons for this. For some it is denial, a misunderstanding of the Scriptures or they just hate change. Whatever the reason, you are going to have to navigate their objections with both reasonable arguments and a bit of emotional appeal.

The point is you will have to talk with the church's official and unofficial leaders. Learn their point of view and try to guide them toward a safer church. You will have some small victories and lose some. But once again, do what you can, even the small things, to safeguard the flock.

The third pitfall overlaps with the second. It is possible that you and your team are not ready to develop an Active Shooter Response program. This is hard to say, but it is possible that you and your team have not gained the trust and credibility of your leaders and congregation. It can be virtually impossible to start a Safety Ministry with Active Shooter Response at the top of the concerns. Many teams have to start with other programs that are easier to sell but are just as important.

For example, it is relatively easy to convince leaders that a Fire Safety and Evacuation program is needed. Most of us grew up practicing fire drills in school and some of us still practice fire drills at work. This makes this program an easy sell.

By starting with an "easy sell" program, you and your team gain trust with parents and leaders. And as time and other "easy sell" programs are implemented, you gain the influence needed to work on your Active Shooter program.

Finally, I want to encourage you to continue doing what you are already doing. Continue to learn as much as you can about safety and security in houses of worship.

Knowledge and training are essential to developing and maintaining a safe church. May God bless you and your efforts.

REFERENCES

The Advanced Law Enforcement Rapid Response Training (ALERRT) Center at Texas State University and the Federal Bureau of Investigation. (2018). *Active shooter incidents in the United States in 2016 and 2017*. Retrieved from https://www.fbi.gov/file-repository/active-shooter-incidents-us-2016-2017.pdf/view

American Crime Prevention Institute. (2012). *The law enforcement officer's complete crime prevention manual* (Vols. 1-2). Goshen, KY: Author.

Bacon, J., and Dearman, E. (2017, November 6). "Domestic situation" linked to Texas church massacre. *USA Today*. Retrieved from https://www.usatoday.com/story/news/nation/2017/11/06/texas-shooters-laws-have-attended-services-targeted-church/835133001/

Blair, J. P., and Schweit, K. W. (2014). *A study of active shooter incidents, 2000-2013*. Texas State University and Federal Bureau of Investigation. Retrieved from https://www.fbi.gov/file-repository/active-shooter-study-2000-2013-1.pdf/view

Burke, D. (2017, November 10). The truth about church shootings. *CNN*. Retrieved from https://www.cnn.com/2017/11/06/us/church-shootings-truth/index.html

Chinn, C. (2018). Ministry violence statistics updated 1/14/18 for period ending 12/31/17. Retrieved from http://www.carlchinn.com/deadly-force-statistics.html

CNN Wire. (2015). Dylann Roof confesses to killing 9 people in Charleston church, wanting to start "race war." Retrieved from http://myfox8.com/2015/06/19/charleston-shooting-suspect-dylan-roof-confesses-to-killing-9-people/

CNN. (2016). Virginia Tech shootings fast facts. *CNN*. Retrieved from http://www.cnn.com/2013/10/31/us/virginia-tech-shootings-fast-facts/

Coleman, N. (2017, August 7). On average, 9 mosques have been targeted every month this year. *CNN*. Retrieved from https://www.cnn.com/2017/03/20/us/mosques-targeted-2017-trnd/index.html

Cooper, T. (2018, March 18). Valley Bible Fellowship church adds armed security guards. *23ABC News*. Retrieved from https://www.turnto23.com/news/local-news/valley-bible-fellowship-church-adds-armed-security-guards

Costa, R., Bever, L., Freedom du Lac, J., and Horwitz, S. (2015, June 18). Church shooting suspect Dylann Roof captured amid hate crime investigation. *Washington Post*. Retrieved from https://www.washingtonpost.com

Crow, K. (2017, November 8). Sutherland Springs: Mass shooters often have domestic violence trait. *USA Today*. Retrieved from https://www.usatoday.com

Defense of others. (2016). National Paralegal College. Retrieved from http://nationalparalegal.edu/public_documents/courseware_asp_files/criminalLaw/defenses/DefenseofOthers.asp

Dorn, M., Dorn, C., Satterly, S., Shepherd, S., and Nguyen, P. (2013). 7 lessons learned from Sandy Hook. *Campus Safety*. Retrieved from https://www.campussafetymagazine.com/safety/7-lessons-learned-from-sandy-hook/

Federal Bureau of Investigation. (n.d.). Officers feloniously killed. *2014 law enforcement officers killed & assaulted*. Retrieved from https://www.fbi.gov/about-us/cjis/ucr/leoka/2014/officers-feloniously-killed

Fox, J. A., and DeLateur, M. J. (2013). Mass shootings in America: Moving beyond Newtown. *Homicide Studies, 18*(1), 125-145.

Fretz, R. A. (2007, November 8). Lessons learned at Virginia Tech shooting. *Police One*. Retrieved from https://www.policeone.com/school-violence/articles/1473536-Lessons-learned-at-Virginia-Tech-shooting/

Goodwyn, W. (2018, March 23). 20 years later, Jonesboro shooting survivors conflicted over Parkland. *National Public Radio*. Retrieved from https://www.npr.org/2018/03/23/596103091/20-years-later-jonesboro-shooting-survivors-conflicted-over-parkland

Grossman, D. (2012, September 11-12). Calibre Press. Training for Law Enforcement [Seminar]. Bloomington, MN.

GuideOne Center for Risk Management. (2018). Church violence. Retrieved from https://www.guideone.com/safety-resources/church-violence

Heath, C. and Heath, D. (2008). *Made to stick: Why some ideas survive and others die.* New York, NY: Random House.

Huffstutler, A. (2018, April 4). UPDATE: Man arrested for breaking into cars at Easter church service. *WRCBtv*. Retrieved from http://www.wrcbtv.com/story/37860294/man-spotted-breaking-into-cars-at-easter-church-service

Hyatt, M. (2018). *Your best year ever: A 5-step plan for achieving your most important goals.* Grand Rapids, MI: Baker Books.

110

Jorge, K., and Ferrier, D. (2018, February 21). Officials say "potential mass shooting thwarted" in middle Tennessee. *News Channel 9 ABC*. Retrieved from http://newschannel9.com/news/local/officials-say-potential-mass-shooting-thwarted-in-middle-tennessee

McRary, A. (2017, December 9). After church shootings, concerned congregations learn to protect their flocks. *Knox News*. Retrieved from https://www.knoxnews.com/story/news/2017/12/10/church-shootings-gun-violence-armed-security-protection-guns/923605001/

Moloney, K. (Author). (2017, November 6). CSRC078: Katie bar the door. [Audio podcast]. *Church Security Roll Call*. Retrieved from https://soundcloud.com/churchsecurityrollcall/

National Institute of Justice. (2009). The use-of-force continuum. Retrieved from http://www.nij.gov/topics/law-enforcement/officer-safety/use-of-force/pages/continuum.aspx

Nicholson, K. (2008, January 17). Church shooter left letter "To God" in car. *Denver Post*. Retrieved from http://www.denverpost.com

Open letter: Don't name them, don't show them. (2017, October 2). Retrieved from https://drive.google.com/file/d/0B4Z7VkWcwLk-SjFJc00tdmI1eW8/view

Pantazi, A., and Crawford, S. (2012, October 29). Forest Hill pastor beaten to death with electric guitar at his church. *Dallas News*. Retrieved from https://www.dallasnews.com/news/crime/2012/10/29/forest-hill-pastor-beaten-to-death-with-electric-guitar-at-his-church

Radiation Emergency Medical Management, U.S. Department of Health & Human Services. (2018). START adult triage algorithm. Retrieved from https://www.remm.nlm.gov/startadult.htm

Randall, M. and DeBoer, H. (2012). The Castle Doctrine and stand-your-ground law. Office of Legislative Research [of Connecticut]. Retrieved from https://www.cga.ct.gov/2012/rpt/2012-R-0172.htm

Reinhart, C. (2007). Castle Doctrine and self-defense. Office of Legislative Research [of Connecticut]. Retrieved from https://www.cga.ct.gov/2007/rpt/2007-R-0052.htm

Ross, B. (2017, December 7). After Sutherland Springs massacre, churches train for active shooters. *USA Today*. Retrieved from https://www.usatoday.com/story/news/nation/2017/12/07/after-sutherland-springs-massacre-churches-train-active-shooters/931103001/

Sanchez, R. and Payne, E. (2015). Charleston church shooting: Who is Dylann Roof? *CNN*. Retrieved from http://www.cnn.com/2015/06/19/us/charleston-church-shooting-suspect/index.html

Schweit, K. W. (2016). *Active shooter incidents in the United States in 2014 and 2015.* Federal Bureau of Investigation, U.S. Department of Justice. Retrieved from https://www.fbi.gov/file-repository/activeshooterincidentsus_2014-2015.pdf/view

Self-defense overview. (2016). FindLaw. Retrieved from http://files.findlaw.com/pdf/criminal/criminal.findlaw.com_criminal-law-basics_self-defense-overview.pdf

Sheepdog Seminars. (2015, March). Sheepdog Seminar. [Seminar]. Shakopee, MN.

Shellnutt, K. (2017, November 7). A top reason for church shootings: Domestic abuse. *Christianity Today*. Retrieved from https://www.christianitytoday.com/news/2017/november/top-reason-church-shooting-domestic-violence-texas.html

State of New Jersey, Assembly No. 159, 213th Legislature. The New Jersey Self-Defense Law. (2008). Retrieved from http://www.njleg.state.nj.us/2008/Bills/A0500/159_I1.pdf

Sterling, J, Lynch, J, and Grinberg, E. (2017, September 26). New details emerge about suspected gunman in Tennessee church shooting. *CNN*. Retrieved from http://www.cnn.com/2017/09/25/us/tennessee-shooting-probe/index.html

Stetzer, E. (2017, November 8). Church security: how do we keep our churches safe in a world where evil is present? *Christianity Today*. Retrieved from https://www.christianitytoday.com/edstetzer/2017/november/church-security-how-do-we-keep-our-people-safe-in-world-whe.html

Towers, S., Gomez-Lievano, A., Khan, M. Mubayi, A., and Castillo-Chavez, C. (2015). Contagion in mass killings and school shootings. *PLOS ONE*. doi: https://doi.org/10.1371/journal.pone.0117259

U.S. church gunman killed himself. (2007, December 12). *BBC News*. Retrieved from http://news.bbc.co.uk

United States Department of Homeland Security. (2008). *Active shooter: How to respond.* Retrieved from https://www.dhs.gov/xlibrary/assets/active_shooter_booklet.pdf

Walfield, S. M., Socia, K. M., and Powers, R. A. (2017) Religious motivated hate crimes: Reporting to law enforcement and case outcomes. *American Journal of Criminal Justice, 42*, 148-169. doi: 10.1007/s12103-016-9349-3

Wootson Jr., C. R. (2017, November 6). The other deadly church shooting in America on Sunday. *Washington Post.* Retrieved from https://www.washingtonpost.com/news/acts-of-faith/wp/2017/11/06/the-other-deadly-church-shooting-in-america-on-sunday/?utm_term=.116bcd0b3eff

112

Made in the USA
Columbia, SC
08 January 2019